STUFFED WAFFLE MAGIC

EFFORTLESS RECIPES USING A STUFFED WAFFLE MAKER

Marilyn Haugen

ISBN: 978-0-9982470-4-5

Stuffed Waffle Magic
Text copyright © 2024 Marilyn Haugen
Photographs copyright © 2024 Marilyn Haugen
Cover and text design copyright © 2024 Marilyn Haugen

No part of this publication may be reproduced, stored in a retrieval system or transmitted, in any form or by any means, without the prior written consent of the publisher and author.

Disclaimer
The recipes in this book have been carefully tested by our kitchen and our tasters. To the best of our knowledge, they are safe and nutritious for ordinary use and users. For those people with food or other allergies, or who have special food requirements or health issues, please read the suggested contents of each recipe carefully and determine whether or not they may create a problem for you. All recipes are used at the risk of the consumer. Consumers should always consult their egg bite maker manufacturer's manual for recommended procedures and cooking times.
We cannot be responsible for any hazards, loss or damage that may occur as a result of any recipe use.
For those with special needs, allergies, requirements or health problems, in the event of any doubt, please contact your medical adviser prior to the use of any recipe.

Published by Emjay Media
Madison, WI

Paperback Edition   Manufactured in the United States of America

Contents

Introduction	7
Getting Started	9
Waffle Batter Recipes	13
Breakfast Waffles	21
Waffles for Dinner	43
International Flavors	67
Desserts	75
Kid-Friendly	86
Seasonal	93
From the Author	102

Introduction

Welcome to the *Stuffed Waffle Magic* cookbook, your ultimate guide to creating delicious and innovative stuffed waffles. Whether you're new to the kitchen or an experienced cook, this book will inspire you with a variety of recipes that transform ordinary waffles into extraordinary meals.

Stuffed waffles are not just for breakfast anymore; they can be enjoyed at any time of the day. From savory to sweet, healthy to indulgent, there's a stuffed waffle for every taste and occasion. These waffles combine the beloved texture of a classic waffle with endless filling possibilities.
In this cookbook, you'll find a range of recipes designed to suit different dietary needs and preferences. I've included vegetarian and vegan options, gluten-free alternatives, and kid-friendly options. Each recipe is easy to follow, with step-by-step instructions and tips to help you achieve the perfect stuffed waffle every time.

The Basics

This cookbook starts with the basics, teaching you how to make a perfect waffle batter. From there, we explore various fillings and combinations, ensuring you have plenty of inspiration to get creative in the kitchen. The breakfast section will jumpstart your day with hearty, protein-packed waffles, with a delightful array of fruity and sweet treats.

Lunch and dinner options bring a new twist to classic meals, and our dessert waffles will satisfy your sweet tooth in the most indulgent way. For those who love meat, the *breakfast for dinner* chapter is packed with rich, flavorful recipes. Seafood enthusiasts will find unique and delicious options there too. Vegetarian, vegan and gluten-free recipes are also in the chapters.

If you're cooking for kids, you'll appreciate the *kid-friendly chapter*, full of fun and tasty recipes that little ones will love.

Explore the international flavors, bringing global cuisine to your waffle iron. From Mexican-inspired waffles to Italian classics, you'll travel the world one bite at a time. Holiday and seasonal waffles offer festive options to celebrate special occasions, making your gatherings even more memorable.

I've provided tips and variations with the individual recipes to help you master the art of stuffed waffles and overcome any challenges you might encounter.

Stuffed waffles are a culinary delight that have gained popularity for their versatility and deliciousness. With the introduction of stuffed waffle makers, crafting these delightful waffles has become so much easier and faster.

What Are Stuffed Waffles?

Stuffed waffles are simply waffles with a filling inside, unlike traditional. This creates a convenient, portable meal that's perfect for any time of day. The fillings can range from savory to sweet, providing endless possibilities for creativity in the kitchen.

Why Stuffed Waffles?

Stuffed waffles offer several advantages over traditional waffles:

- Convenience: All the ingredients are contained within the waffle, making it easy to eat on the go.
- Variety: The range of possible fillings means you can enjoy different flavors and textures in each bite.
- Balance: Combining proteins, vegetables, and carbohydrates in one dish makes for a balanced meal.
- Fun: Creating and eating stuffed waffles is an enjoyable experience for both adults and kids.

Getting Started

To start making stuffed waffles, you'll need a few basic tools:

- Stuffed Waffle Maker: A good-quality stuffed waffle maker is essential. Choose one with an overflow area to avoid your ingredients oozing out the sides of the maker.
- Mixing Bowls: You'll need bowls for mixing the batter and preparing the fillings.
- Whisk and Spatula: These are useful for mixing and handling the batter.

In the following chapters, we'll guide you through the process of making different types of stuffed waffles, from the basics to more advanced recipes. You'll learn how to create perfect batters, select the best fillings, and cook your waffles to perfection. Let's embark on this delicious journey and discover the endless possibilities of stuffed waffles!

Tips for Perfect Stuffed Waffles

To help you master the art of stuffed waffles, this section provides tips, tricks, and troubleshooting advice. I've summarized many of my top tips for making perfect stuffed waffles.

Always refer to your specific manufacturer's instructions.

- Preheat Your Waffle Iron: Always preheat your waffle iron to ensure even cooking and a crispy exterior.
- Don't Overfill: Be careful not to overfill your waffle iron with batter and fillings to avoid overflow and uneven cooking.
- Use Non-Stick Spray: Lightly spray your waffle iron with non-stick cooking spray, if needed, to prevent sticking.
- Check for Doneness: Cook your waffles until they are golden brown and crisp. If unsure, carefully open the waffle iron to check.

Troubleshooting Common Issues

- Waffles Sticking to the Iron: Ensure your waffle iron is properly preheated and lightly greased. If sticking persists, try a different batter recipe.
- Uneven Cooking: Make sure to spread the batter evenly over the waffle iron and avoid overfilling.
- Overflow: Use the right amount of batter and fillings, and do not overfill the waffle iron.
- Soggy Waffles: Cook your waffles until they are crispy and golden brown. If they are still soggy, close the waffle maker and cook them for a few minutes longer.

With these tips and recipes, you'll be well-equipped to create delicious and creative stuffed waffles for any occasion. Enjoy exploring the endless possibilities of stuffed waffles!

Thank you for choosing *Stuffed Waffle Magic*. I hope you have fun making them and that it inspires you to create delicious, memorable meals for yourself and your loved ones. Happy cooking!

Waffle Batter Recipes

Homestyle Belgian Waffle Batter   14
Classic Buttermilk Waffle Batter   15
Cornmeal Waffle Batter   16
Gluten Free Waffle Batter   17
Vegan Chickpea Waffles   18

Homestyle Belgian Waffle Batter

The Belgian waffle batter is simple and versatile, making it perfect for both savory and sweet stuffed waffles. The result is a well-recognized and comforting waffle.

Makes 3 to 4 Stuffed Waffles

1-1/2 cups	all-purpose flour
1-1/2 tsp	baking powder
4-1/2 tsp	granulated sugar
1/4 tsp	salt
1	large egg, separated
2 cups	milk
1/4 cup	vegetable oil
1/2 tsp	vanilla extract

1. In a large bowl, whisk together flour, baking powder, sugar and salt.
2. In a medium bowl, whisk together the egg yolks, milk, vegetable oil and vanilla until blended. Pour over flour mixture and stir just until smooth.
3. In another medium bowl, using an electric mixer, beat egg whites with a pinch of salt until stiff peaks form.
4. Fold one-third of the egg whites into the batter until blended. Gently fold in the remaining egg whites just until no white streaks remain.
5. Continue with the stuffed waffle recipe of your choice.

Tips

* If making and serving more than one stuffed waffle, preheat oven to 200°F. Transfer cooked waffle to a wire rank on a baking sheet. Keep warm in oven until all waffles are cooked.
* Leftover waffle batter can be refrigerated in an airtight container for up to 3 days or frozen for up to 3 months.
* To freeze cooked waffles, let them cool completely. Then transfer them to an airtight container. Cooked waffles can be frozen for up to 3 months.

Classic Buttermilk Waffle Batter

A classic and delicious buttermilk waffle is a breakfast treat known for its light, airy texture and slight tang from the buttermilk.

Makes 3 to 4 Stuffed Waffles

1-1 /2 cups	all-purpose flour
1-2 1 tsp	baking powder
1/2 tsp	baking soda
	Table salt
3	large eggs, separated
2 tsp	granulated sugar
1-2/3 cups	buttermilk
2 tbsp	butter, melted or vegetable oil
	Nonstick cooking spray

1. In a large bowl, whisk together flour, baking powder, baking soda and 1/2 tsp salt.
2. In a medium bowl, whisk together the egg yolks, sugar, buttermilk and butter until blended. Pour over flour mixture and stir just until smooth.
3. In another medium bowl, using an electric mixer, beat egg whites with a pinch of salt until stiff peaks form.
4. Fold one-third of the egg whites into the batter until blended. Then gently fold in the remaining egg whites just until no white streaks remain.
5. Continue with the stuffed waffle recipe of your choice.

Tips
* If making and serving more than one stuffed waffle, preheat oven to 200°F. Transfer cooked waffle to a wire rank on a baking sheet. Keep warm in oven until all waffles are cooked.
* Leftover waffle batter can be refrigerated in an airtight container for up to 3 days. The batter can be frozen in an airtight container for up to 3 months.

Cornmeal Waffle Batter

Cornmeal waffles incorporate cornmeal for a hearty texture and a subtly sweet corn flavor. The waffles have a pleasant crunch and golden color.

Makes 3 to 4 Stuffed Waffles

1 cup	all-purpose flour
1 cup	cornmeal
1-1	/2 tsp baking powder
1/2 tsp	baking soda salt
1	large eggs, separated
2 tsp	granulated sugar
1-3/4 cups	buttermilk
1/4 cup	butter, melted or vegetable oil

Nonstick cooking spray

1. In a large bowl, whisk together flour, cornmeal, baking powder, baking soda and 1 tsp salt.
2. In a medium bowl, whisk together the egg yolks, sugar, buttermilk and butter until blended. Pour over flour mixture and stir just until smooth.
3. In another medium bowl, using an electric mixer, beat egg whites with a pinch of salt until stiff peaks form.
4. Fold one-third of the egg whites into the batter until blended. Then gently fold in the remaining egg whites just until no white streaks remain.
5. Continue with the stuffed waffle recipe of choice.

Tips
* If making and serving more than one stuffed waffle, preheat oven to 200°F. Transfer cooked waffle to a wire rank on a baking sheet. Keep warm in oven until all waffles are cooked.
* Leftover waffle batter can be refrigerated in an airtight container for up to 3 days. The batter can be frozen in an airtight container for up to 3 months.

Gluten Free Waffle Batter

Gluten-free waffle batter is made using alternative flours to avoid wheat. This batter ensures a light and fluffy texture, accommodating those with gluten sensitivities without sacrificing taste

Makes 3 to 4 Stuffed Waffles

1-1/2 cups	gluten free all-purpose flour
1 tbsp	granulated sugar
2 tsp	baking powder
1/2 tsp	baking soda Salt
3/4 cup	milk
4	large eggs, separated
1 tbsp	vegetable oil
1 tsp	vanilla extract

1. In a large bowl, whisk together flour, sugar, baking powder, baking soda and 1/2 tsp salt.
2. In a medium bowl, whisk together the milk, egg yolks, vanilla and oil. Pour over flour mixture and stir just until smooth.
3. In another medium bowl, using an electric mixer, beat egg whites with a pinch of salt until stiff peaks form.
4. Fold one-third of the egg whites into the batter until blended. Then gently fold in the remaining egg whites just until no white streaks remain.
5. Continue with the stuffed waffle recipe of choice.

Tips
* If making and serving more than one stuffed waffle, preheat oven to 200°F. Transfer cooked waffle to a wire rank on a baking sheet. Keep warm in oven until all waffles are cooked.
* Leftover waffle batter can be refrigerated in an airtight container for up to 3 days. The batter can be frozen in an airtight container for up to 3 months.

Vegan Chickpea Waffles

Vegan waffle batter made with chickpeas utilizes chickpea flour, offering a protein-rich and egg-free alternative. This batter provides a slightly nutty flavor and a sturdy texture, perfect for a satisfying vegan breakfast.

Makes 3 to 4 Stuffed Waffles

1	cups chickpea flour
2 tsp	baking powder
Pinch	salt
1 cup	water

1. In a mixing bowl, combine chickpea flour, baking powder and salt; mixing well.
2. Add water and whisk until the batter is relatively smooth.
3. Let the batter rest for 15 minutes.
4. Continue with the stuffed waffle recipe of choice.

Tip
* Batter should be thick, but still pourable. If the batter is too thick, add 1 tsp of water at a time until the batter reaches pourable consistency.

Breakfast Waffles

McWaffle Stuffed Egg Sandwich	23
Country-Style Stuffed Breakfast Waffle	25
Sausage Patty, Egg, and Cheese Stuffed Waffle	27
Southern Sausage and Gravy Stuffed Biscuits	29
Bacon, Sun-dried Tomatoes and Spinach	31
Canadian Bacon, Spinach and Swiss	32
Everything Bagel Stuffed Waffles	33
Spicy Avocado Stuffed Waffle	35
Refreshing Blueberry Cream Cheese	37
Hazelnut Banana Stuffed Waffle	39
Triple Berry Stuffed Waffle	40
Monkey Bread Waffle	41

McWaffle Stuffed Egg Sandwich

Experience the delight of a sandwich and a waffle in one, featuring a perfectly cooked egg nestled between crisp waffle layers.
Makes 1

2/3 cup	prepared all-purpose baking mix
1	large egg, fried
2	slices cheddar cheese
3	thin slices deli ham Maple syrup (optional)

1. Preheat waffle maker.
2. Prepare baking mix as directed on the package.
3. Spray waffle maker with cooking spray. Ladle about 1/3 cup batter into waffle maker, spreading batter so the bottom grids and waffle divider are thinly but completely covered.
4. Place the fried egg onto batter leaving a thin margin around edge. Place 2 slices of cheese on the egg and add 2 slices of ham onto the top.
5. Pour the remaining batter on top of the filling and along the sides.
6. Close waffle maker and flip. Cook until golden brown and crisp, about 7 to 8 minutes.
7. Transfer the stuffed waffle to a plate. Serve with maple syrup, if desired.

Tip
* A scrambled egg can be substituted for the fried egg. Cook according to your desired doneness.

Country-Style Stuffed Breakfast Waffle

Kickstart your morning with a hearty waffle stuffed with traditional country ingredients, perfect for a fulfilling start.

Makes 2 to 3

1-1/2 cups	frozen tater tots, defrosted
2	eggs
2 tsp	butter
2	breakfast sausage links, cooked and chopped
2 tbsp	grated cheddar cheese

1. Preheat waffle maker.
2. Meanwhile, crumble the tater tots into a mixing bowl. Add one egg and stir until combined. Set aside.
3. In a small skillet over medium heat add the butter and cook until melted. Add the remaining egg and cook to your liking.
4. Spray the preheated waffle maker with cooking spray. Ladle about one half the tater mixture into the waffle maker making sure to cover the sides and edges.
5. Scatter the chopped sausages evenly over the top of the tater tots. Add the fried egg on top of the sausages. Sprinkle with the grated cheddar cheese. Top with remaining tater tot mixture.
6. Close waffle maker and flip. Cook until golden brown and crisp, about 8 to 10 minutes. Transfer the stuffed waffle to a plate.

Sausage Patty, Egg, and Cheese Stuffed Waffle

Dive into a savory waffle stuffed with sausage, egg, and melted cheese, offering a complete breakfast in each bite.

Makes 1 stuffed waffle

2/3 cup	prepared all-purpose baking mix
1	egg, scrambled
2	slices cheddar cheese
2	cooked breakfast sausage patties (about 1/4-inch thick)

1. Preheat waffle maker.
2. Prepare baking mix as directed on package.
3. Spray waffle maker with cooking spray. Ladle about 1/3 cup batter into waffle maker, spreading batter so the bottom grids and waffle divider are thinly but completely covered.
4. Spoon scrambled eggs onto batter leaving a thin margin around edge. Place cheese slices over egg. Add sausage patties over cheese. Spread additional batter over filling until it reaches the top of the square projections on the waffle tongs.
5. Close the waffle maker and flip. Cook until golden brown and crisp, about 7 to 8 minutes.
6. Transfer the stuffed waffle to a plate.

Tips
* Yields may vary depending upon the baking mix used. You will need about 2/3 cup batter for 1 stuffed waffle. You can adjust the filling according.
* Leftover waffle batter can be refrigerated in an airtight container for up to 3 days.

Southern Sausage and Gravy Stuffed Biscuits

Savor the taste of the South with these biscuits bursting with sausage and rich, creamy gravy.

Makes 4

1	tube refrigerated buttermilk biscuits
1 lb	bulk pork sausage
2 tbsp	all-purpose flour
1/4 tsp	black pepper
1/4 tsp	garlic powder
1/4 tsp	onion powder
1/4 tsp	ground sage
1 cup	milk

1. Preheat waffle maker. Preheat oven to 200°F.
2. Meanwhile, in large skillet over medium heat, brown sausage, breaking up into chunks as it cooks. Do not drain fat. Reduce heat to low and stir in flour, pepper, garlic powder, onion powder and ground sage. Stir until mixture evenly coats sausage. Add milk and stir until thickened. Remove from heat.
3. Open the refrigerated biscuit tube and separate biscuits into 8 pieces. Stretch biscuits into large circles to fit inside the waffle maker and up the sides.
4. Carefully add 1 biscuit round into the waffle maker, using silicone tongs to stretch the round up the sides of the maker. Spoon 1/3 cup sausage and gravy filling onto biscuit leaving a thin margin around edge. Add an additional biscuit over the filling so it reaches the edge of the waffle maker covering the filling.
5. Place the first stuffed waffle on a baking rack on a sheet pan and put in the oven to keep warm. Repeat with remaining ingredients spraying with cooking spray in between. Transfer the stuffed waffles to plates. Cut into quarters, if desired and serve with any remaining sausage gravy.

Tip

* You can refrigerate cooked stuffed waffles in a tightly sealed container in the refrigerator up to 3 days

Bacon, Sun-dried Tomatoes and Spinach Stuffed Waffle

Enjoy a waffle filled with the robust flavors of bacon, sun-dried tomatoes, and spinach for a satisfying meal.

Makes 1

2/3 cup	Homestyle Belgian Waffle Batter
3 slices	cooked bacon
3 tbsp	sun-dried tomatoes packed in oil, julienne cut
	Fresh baby spinach leaves

1. Preheat waffle maker.
2. Spray waffle maker with cooking spray. Ladle about 1/3 cup batter into waffle maker, spreading batter so the bottom grids and waffle divider are thinly but completely covered.
3. Arrange bacon slices onto waffle batter, breaking as needed to leave a slim margin around the edge. Arrange sun dried tomatoes and a single layer of spinach leaves over the top of the bacon.
4. Spread additional batter over filling until it reaches the top of the square projections on the waffle tongs. Close waffle maker and flip. Cook for 7 to 8 minutes.
5. Transfer stuffed waffle to a plate.

Tip
* Leftover waffle batter can be refrigerated in an airtight container for up to 3 days.

Canadian Bacon, Spinach and Swiss Stuffed Waffle

Indulge in the smooth blend of Canadian bacon, spinach, and Swiss cheese, all stuffed into a fluffy waffle.

Makes 1

2/3 cup	Homestyle Belgian Waffle Batter
	Spinach leaves
1 tsp	Dijon mustard
2 slices	Canadian bacon
2 slices	Swiss cheese

1. Preheat waffle maker.
2. Spray waffle maker with cooking spray. Ladle about 1/3 cup batter into waffle maker, spreading batter so the bottom grids and waffle divider are thinly but completely covered.
3. Arrange spinach leaves in an even layer onto batter leaving a thin margin around edge. Spread Dijon mustard on one side of each slice of Canadian bacon. Cut bacon in half and arrange on top of spinach leaves. Add Swish cheese to the top.
4. Spread additional batter over filling until it reaches the top of the square projections on the waffle tongs. Close waffle maker and flip. Cook for 7 to 8 minutes.
5. Transfer stuffed waffle to a plate. Serve with additional Dijon mustard, if desired.

Monkey Bread Waffle

Treat yourself to a sweet escape with a waffle that captures the gooey, cinnamon-laced magic of monkey bread.

Makes 2

1 tube	refrigerated cinnamon buns
1/4 cup	diced apples
3 tbsp	raisins
3 tbsp	chopped pecans

1. Preheat waffle maker. Preheat oven to 200°F.
2. Open the tube of cinnamon buns. Remove the glaze packet and set aside. Divide the dough into 4 sections. Form dough into circles that will fit inside the waffle maker.
3. In a small bowl, combine the apples, raisins and pecans.
4. Carefully add one dough round to the stuffed waffle maker. Use a silicone spatula to spread the dough into the mold and up the edges.
5. Spoon one-half of the apple mixture on top of the dough. Top with one dough round. Close waffle maker and flip. Cook for 7 to 8 minutes.
6. Place the waffle on a baking rack on a sheet pan and put in the oven to keep warm. Repeat with remaining ingredients spraying with cooking spray in between.
7. Transfer stuffed waffles to plates. Serve drizzled with the reserved glaze.

Spicy Avocado Stuffed Waffle

Spice up your breakfast with a waffle stuffed with creamy avocado with a kick, combining taste and texture perfectly.

Makes 1

2/3 cup	prepared all-purpose baking mix
1	egg, scrambled
2 slices	pepperjack cheese
5 slices	avocado Salsa, optional

1. Preheat waffle maker.
2. Prepare baking mix as directed on package.
3. Spray waffle maker with cooking spray. Ladle about 1/3 cup batter into waffle maker, spreading batter so the bottom grids and waffle divider are thinly but completely covered.
4. Spoon scrambled eggs onto batter leaving a thin margin around edge. Place cheese slices over scrambled eggs and top with avocado slices.
5. Spread additional batter over filling until it reaches the top of the square projections on the waffle tongs. Close waffle maker and flip. Cook for 7 to 8 minutes.
6. Transfer stuffed waffle to a plate. Serve with a spoonful of salsa, if using.

Tips
* Yields may vary depending upon the baking mix used. You will need about 2/3 cup batter for the 1 stuffed waffle. You can adjust the filling accordingly.
* Leftover waffle batter can be refrigerated in an airtight container for up to 3 days.

Refreshing Blueberry Cream Cheese Stuffed Waffle

Delight in the burst of fresh blueberries and creamy cheese in this refreshing, sweet waffle.

Makes 1

2/3 cup	prepared Homestyle Buttermilk Waffles
1/3 cup	fresh blueberries*
1 oz	cream cheese, cut into small pieces

1. Preheat waffle maker.
2. Spray waffle maker with cooking spray. Ladle about 1/3 cup batter into waffle maker, spreading batter so the bottom grids and waffle divider are thinly but completely covered.
3. Arrange fresh blueberries and cream cheese pieces in an even layer onto batter leaving a thin margin around edge.
4. Spread additional batter over filling until it reaches the top of the square projections on the waffle tongs. Close waffle maker and flip. Cook for 7 to 8 minutes.
5. Transfer stuffed waffle to a plate. Cut waffles into wedges and serve.

Tip
* Frozen blueberries can be used in place of fresh blueberries. Defrost and drain berries before using.

Hazelnut Banana Stuffed Waffle

Relish a waffle filled with the nutty sweetness of hazelnuts and bananas for a decadent breakfast or dessert.

Makes 1

2/3 cup	prepared package of pancake and waffle mix
2 tbsp	hazelnut spread
1	banana, sliced

1. Preheat waffle maker.
2. Prepare pancake and waffle mix as directed on the package.
3. Spray waffle maker with cooking spray. Ladle 1/3 cup batter into waffle maker, spreading batter so the bottom grids and waffle divider are thinly but completely covered.
4. Spoon the hazelnut spread on to the batter. Add the sliced bananas in a single layer over the top of the spread and within 1/4 inch of the edge of the batter. Set aside the remaining banana.
5. Ladle additional batter over the filling until it reaches the top of the square projections on the waffle tongs.
6. Close the waffle maker and flip. Cook until golden brown and crisp, about 7 to 8 minutes.
7. Transfer the stuffed waffle to a plate. Serve remaining sliced bananas on top or on the side.

Tips
* Yields may vary depending upon the pancake and waffle mix used.
* Leftover waffle batter can be refrigerated in an airtight container for up to 3 days.
* Serve the remaining sliced bananas with sliced strawberries.

Triple Berry Stuffed Waffle

Enjoy a berry-packed waffle stuffed with a mix of strawberries, blueberries, and raspberries, bursting with natural sweetness.

Makes 1

2/3 cup	Classic Buttermilk Waffle Batter
1 tbsp	chopped pecans
1/2 tbsp	packed brown sugar
1/2 cup	fresh or frozen, drained, mixed berries (blueberries, raspberries, and blackberries)
	Maple syrup for serving (optional)

1. Preheat waffle maker.
2. Stir the chopped pecans and the brown sugar into the 2/3 cup of prepared buttermilk waffle batter.
3. Spray waffle maker with cooking spray. Ladle about 1/3 cup batter into waffle maker, spreading batter so the bottom grids and waffle divider are thinly but completely covered.
4. Spoon mixed berries onto batter leaving a thin margin around edge.
5. Spread additional batter over filling until it reaches the top of the square projections on the waffle tongs. Close waffle maker and flip. Cook for 6-1/2 to 8 minutes.
6. Transfer stuffed waffle to a plate. Serve with maple syrup, if using.

Tip
* Leftover waffle batter can be refrigerated in an airtight container for up to 3 days.

Monkey Bread Waffle

Treat yourself to a sweet escape with a waffle that captures the gooey, cinnamon- laced magic of monkey bread.

Makes 2

1 tube	refrigerated cinnamon buns
1/4 cup	diced apples
3 tbsp	raisins
3 tbsp	chopped pecans

1. Preheat waffle maker. Preheat oven to 200°F.
2. Open the tube of cinnamon buns. Remove the glaze packet and set aside. Divide the dough into 4 sections. Form dough into circles that will fit inside the waffle maker.
3. In a small bowl, combine the apples, raisins and pecans.
4. Carefully add one dough round to the stuffed waffle maker. Use a silicone spatula to spread the dough into the mold and up the edges.
5. Spoon one-half of the apple mixture on top of the dough. Top with one dough round. Close waffle maker and flip. Cook for 7 to 8 minutes.
6. Place the waffle on a baking rack on a sheet pan and put in the oven to keep warm. Repeat with remaining ingredients spraying with cooking spray in between.
7. Transfer stuffed waffles to plates. Serve drizzled with the reserved glaze.

Waffles for Dinner

Fried Chicken Stuffed Waffles	45
Grilled Cheese with Bacon and Tomatoes	47
Pepperoni Pizza Stuffed Waffles	49
Reuben Stuffed Waffle	50
Spinach Artichoke Stuffed Waffle	51
Bacon, Date, and Feta Cheese Stuffed Waffle	52
Buffalo Chicken Stuffed Waffle	53
Firehouse Chili and Cheese Stuffed Waffle	55
Pulled Pork Stuffed Waffle	56
Halftime BBQ Chicken Stuffed Waffle	57
Chicken Bistro Waffle	59
Hawaiian Pizza Stuffed Waffle	61
Philly Cheesesteak-Inspired Stuffed Waffles	62
Monte Cristo Waffle Stuffers	63
Chicken Pot Pie Waffle	65
Tuna Melt with Tomato Stuffed Waffle	66

Fried Chicken Stuffed Waffles

Makes 1 Stuffed Waffle

2/3 cup	Classic Buttermilk Waffle Batter
2	crispy chicken strips (about 1.5 to 2 oz each), cooked
1 tbsp	honey
	Additional honey for serving

1. Preheat the waffle maker.
2. Prepare Classic Buttermilk Waffle Batter as directed in steps 1 to 4.
3. Spray waffle maker with cooking spray. Ladle about 1/3 cup batter into waffle maker, spreading batter so the bottom grids and waffle divider are thinly but completely covered.
4. Place chicken strips onto the batter, cutting as needed to fit and leave a thin margin around edge. Drizzle 1 tbsp honey over chicken strips.
5. Ladle additional batter over chicken filling until it reaches the top of the square projections on the waffle tongs/divider.
6. Close waffle maker and flip. Cook until golden brown and crisp, about 7 to 8 minutes. Transfer the stuffed waffle to a plate.
7. Cut the waffle into quarters. Serve with additional honey.

Variation
* Toss the chicken strip chunks in 3 tbsp of buffalo sauce and omit the honey. Add the chicken chunks on top of the batter as directed. Serve with ranch or blue cheese dressing for dipping.

Tip
* Waffle, pancake, or all-purpose baking mixes can be substituted for Classic Buttermilk Waffle Batter recipe. Prepare as directed on package. Yield may vary depending on the mix used.

Grilled Cheese Stuffed Waffle with Bacon and Tomatoes

Makes 1

2/3 cup	prepared Classic Waffle Batter
2 slices	cooked bacon
1/4 cup	chopped tomatoes
2 slices	cheddar cheese

1. Preheat waffle maker.
2. Spray waffle maker with cooking spray. Ladle about 1/3 cup batter into waffle maker, spreading batter so the bottom grids and waffle divider are thinly but completely covered.
3. Arrange bacon slices onto waffle batter, breaking as needed to leave a slim margin around the edge. Arrange the chopped tomatoes and the 2 slices of cheddar leaving a slim margin around the edge.
4. Spread additional batter over filling until it reaches the top of the square projections on the waffle tongs. Close waffle maker and flip. Cook for 7 to 8 minutes.
5. Transfer stuffed waffle to a plate.

Variation
* Use 2 slices of deli ham, chicken or turkey in place of the bacon.

Tip
* Leftover waffle batter can be refrigerated in an airtight container for up to 3 days.

Pepperoni Pizza Stuffed Waffles

Makes 2

1 tube	refrigerated pizza dough (approx. 12 oz.) or 12 oz fresh pizza dough ball
12 slices	pepperoni
4 tbsp	pizza sauce
3 tbsp	shredded mozzarella cheese
	Additional pizza sauce for dipping

1. Preheat waffle maker. Preheat oven to 200°F.
2. Spray waffle maker with cooking spray.
3. Divide pizza dough into 2 sections. Mold the dough halves into round pieces that will fit into the bottom and up the sides of the waffle maker.
4. Carefully add one pizza dough round to the stuffed waffle maker. Use a silicone spatula to spread the dough into the mold and up the edges.
5. Arrange six slices of pepperoni over the dough, leaving a small space near the edges. Spoon 2 tbsp pizza sauce and 1-1/2 tbsp shredded cheese over the pepperoni.
6. Place the remaining dough circle on top of the filling and far enough to the edge so the waffle will seal when the maker is closed.
7. Close waffle maker and flip. Cook until golden brown and crisp, about 8 to 10 minutes.
8. Place the first pizza waffle on a baking rack on a sheet pan and put in the oven to keep warm. Repeat with remaining ingredients spraying with cooking spray in between.
9. Transfer the stuffed waffles to a plate. Cut into quarters, if desired and serve with pizza sauce for dipping.

Tip
* A 14 ounce jar of pizza sauce will yield about 1-3/4 cups or 29 tbsp. A 15 ounce can will yield about 31 tbsp. Leftover pizza sauce can be stored in a tightly sealed container in the refrigerator for 5 to 7 days.

Reuben Stuffed Waffle

Makes 1

2/3 cup	Cornmeal Waffle Batter
1 slice	Swiss cheese
2 tbsp	drained sauerkraut
1 slice	corned beef
	Thousand Island dressing, for serving

1. Preheat waffle maker.
2. Spray waffle maker with cooking spray. Ladle about 1/3 cup batter into waffle maker, spreading batter so the bottom grids and waffle divider are thinly but completely covered.
3. Place Swiss cheese on top of the batter leaving a thin margin around edge. Spoon the sauerkraut on top of the cheese. Top with the corned beef.
4. Spread additional batter over filling until it reaches the top of the square projections on the waffle tongs. Close waffle maker and flip. Cook for 7 to 8 minutes.
5. Transfer stuffed waffle to a plate. Serve with Thousand Island dressing for dipping.

Spinach Artichoke Stuffed Waffle

Makes 1

2/3 cup	Classic Belgian Waffle Batter
1/3 cup	prepared spinach artichoke dip
2 slices	mozzarella cheese

1. Preheat waffle maker.
2. Spray waffle maker with cooking spray. Ladle about 1/3 cup batter into waffle maker, spreading batter so the bottom grids and waffle divider are thinly but completely covered.
3. Spoon spinach artichoke dip on top of the batter leaving a thin margin around edge. Arrange the mozzarella slices on top.
4. Spread additional batter over filling until it reaches the top of the square projections on the waffle tongs. Close waffle maker and flip. Cook for 7 to 8 minutes.
5. Transfer stuffed waffle to a plate. Serve with Thousand Island dressing for dipping.

Bacon, Date, and Feta Cheese Stuffed Waffle

Makes 1

2/3 cup	Classic Waffle Batter
2 slices	cooked bacon
1/4 cup	chopped dates
2 tbsp	crumbled feta cheese

1. Preheat waffle maker.
2. Spray waffle maker with cooking spray. Ladle about 1/3 cup batter into waffle maker, spreading batter so the bottom grids and waffle divider are thinly but completely covered.
3. Arrange cooked bacon and chopped dates on top of the batter leaving a thin margin around edge. Sprinkle with feta cheese.
4. Spread additional batter over filling until it reaches the top of the square projections on the waffle tongs. Close waffle maker and flip. Cook for 7 to 8 minutes.
5. Transfer stuffed waffle to a plate.

Tip

* Waffle, pancake, or all-purpose baking mixes can be substituted for Classic Waffle Batter recipe. Prepare as directed on package. Yield may vary depending on the mix used.

Buffalo Chicken Stuffed Waffle

Makes 1

2/3 cup	Homestyle Belgian Waffle Batter
2	pieces cooked popcorn chicken
1 tsp	buffalo wing sauce
1 tsp	crumbled blue cheese
	Ranch or blue cheese dressing (optional)

1. Preheat waffle maker.
2. Spray waffle maker with cooking spray. Ladle about 1/3 cup batter into waffle maker, spreading batter so the bottom grids and waffle divider are thinly but completely covered.
3. Cut popcorn chicken into chunks that fit in a shallow layer on top of the batter leaving a thin margin around edge. Drizzle buffalo wing sauce and sprinkle blue cheese over the top.
4. Spread additional batter over filling until it reaches the top of the square projections on the waffle tongs. Close waffle maker and flip. Cook for 7 to 8 minutes.
5. Transfer stuffed waffle to a plate. Serve with ranch or blue cheese dressing, if using.

Tip
* Place the chicken chunks into a small bowl, add the buffalo sauce and then toss gently to coat the chicken.

Firehouse Chili and Cheese Stuffed Waffle

Makes 1

2/3 cup	Cornmeal Waffle Batter
2 tsp	sliced green onions
2	slices cheddar cheese
1/2 cup	chili, homemade or canned

1. Preheat waffle maker.
2. Stir sliced green onions into waffle batter. Spray waffle maker with cooking spray. Ladle about 1/3 cup batter into waffle maker, spreading batter so the bottom grids and waffle divider are thinly but completely covered.
3. Add cheddar cheese, cutting to fit so there is a thin margin near the edge of the batter. Spoon chili on top of the cheese.
4. Spread additional batter over filling until it reaches the top of the square projections on the waffle tongs. Close waffle maker and flip. Cook for 7 to 8 minutes.
5. Transfer stuffed waffle to a plate.

Pulled Pork Stuffed Waffle

Makes 1

2/3 cup	Classic Belgian Waffle Batter
1/2 cup	pulled pork, warmed
1 tbsp	BBQ sauce
1/2 cup	coleslaw (optional)

1. Preheat waffle maker.
2. Spray waffle maker with cooking spray. Ladle about 1/3 cup batter into waffle maker, spreading batter so the bottom grids and waffle divider are thinly but completely covered.
3. Add pulled pork to the top of the dough leaving a thin margin near the edge of the batter. Drizzle BBQ sauce on the top.
4. Spread additional batter over filling until it reaches the top of the square projections on the waffle tongs. Close waffle maker and flip. Cook for 7 to 8 minutes.
5. Transfer stuffed waffle to a plate. Serve topped with coleslaw, if using.

Variation

* Use prepared BBQ pulled pork and omit the additional BBQ sauce.

Halftime BBQ Chicken Stuffed Waffle

Makes 1

2/3 cup	prepared package of pancake and waffle mix 1 tsp garlic powder
1/4 cup	shredded rotisserie chicken
2 tbsp	BBQ sauce
1 tbsp	diced jalapeño pepper

1. Preheat waffle maker.
2. In a small bowl, combine shredded chicken, BBQ sauce and diced jalapeño pepper.
3. Spray waffle maker with cooking spray. Ladle about 1/3 cup batter into waffle maker, spreading batter so the bottom grids and waffle divider are thinly but completely covered.
4. Add shredded to the top of the dough leaving a thin margin near the edge of the batter.
5. Spread additional batter over filling until it reaches the top of the square projections on the waffle tongs. Close waffle maker and flip. Cook for 7 to 8 minutes.
6. Transfer stuffed waffle to a plate. Cut in half for hearty sandwiches or cut into quarters for appetizers and snacks.

Tips
* Yields may vary depending upon the pancake and waffle mix used.
* Leftover waffle batter can be refrigerated in an airtight container for up to 3 days.

Chicken Bistro Waffle

Makes 2 waffles

1 tube	refrigerated crescent dough
1/2 cup	cooked diced chicken breast
1/4 cup	finely chopped roasted red pepper
1/4 cup	grated Italian cheese blend

1. Preheat waffle maker. Preheat oven to 200°F.
2. In a medium bowl, combine the chicken breast, roasted red pepper and the grated Italian cheese blend.
3. Open the refrigerated crescent roll tube and separate dough into 4 sections. Stretch each section into large circles to fit inside the waffle maker and up the sides.
4. Carefully add 1 crescent round into the waffle maker, using silicone tongs to stretch the round up the sides of the maker.
5. Add 1/2 cup of the chicken mixture to the top of the dough.
6. Add another crescent dough round to the top, stretching as needed to cover the edges. Close waffle maker and flip. Cook for 7 to 8 minutes.
7. Place the first stuffed waffle on a baking rack on a sheet pan and put in the oven to keep warm. Repeat with remaining ingredients spraying with cooking spray in between batches, if necessary.
8. Transfer the stuffed waffles to plates. Cut each in half and serve.

Hawaiian Pizza Stuffed Waffle

Makes 2

1 tube	refrigerated pizza dough
4 tsp	pizza sauce
1/2 cup	cooked diced ham
6 tbsp	diced pineapple
1/4 cup	grated mozzarella cheese

1. Preheat waffle maker. Preheat oven to 200°F.
2. Open the refrigerated pizza dough tube and cut dough into 4 equal sections. Stretch each section into large circles to fit inside the waffle maker and up the sides.
3. Carefully add 1 crescent round into the waffle maker, using silicone tongs to stretch the round up the sides of the maker.
4. On top of the dough, add 2 tsp pizza sauce. Using the back of a spoon, spread the sauce over the bottom of the dough. Scatter 1/4 cup ham and 3 tbsp diced pineapple over the sauce. Sprinkle with 2 tbsp mozzarella cheese.
5. Add another pizza dough round to the top, stretching as needed to cover the edges. Close waffle maker and flip. Cook for 7 to 8 minutes.
6. Place the first stuffed waffle on a baking rack on a sheet pan and put in the oven to keep warm. Repeat with remaining ingredients spraying with cooking spray in between batches, if necessary.
7. Transfer the stuffed waffles to plates. Cut each in half or quarters and serve.

Monte Cristo Waffle Stuffers

Makes 1

2	eggs
1/2 cup	milk
1/4 tsp	table salt
1/8 tsp	ground black pepper
4	slices white bread
2	slices Swiss cheese
2	thin slices ham
	Powdered sugar (optional for serving) Raspberry jam (optional for serving)

1. Preheat waffle maker.
2. In a medium bowl, whisk the eggs, milk, salt, and black pepper until combined.
3. Dip the bread into the egg batter until fully coated.
4. Place 2 bread slices in the appliance, covering the bottom of the appliance. Layer the cheese and ham on top of the bread. Top with the remaining 2 bread slices.
5. Close waffle maker and flip. Cook for 7 to 8 minutes.
6. Transfer stuffed waffle to a plate. Serve sprinkled with powdered sugar and raspberry jam for dipping.

Philly Cheesesteak-Inspired Stuffed Waffles

Makes 2 waffles

1 tube	refrigerated crescent dough
1/2 cup	thinly sliced cooked sandwich steak 6 tbsp sautéed sliced onions and peppers
1/4 cup	grated Italian cheese blend

1. Preheat waffle maker. Preheat oven to 200°F.
2. Open the refrigerated crescent roll tube and separate dough into 4 sections. Stretch each section into large circles to fit inside the waffle maker and up the sides.
3. Carefully add 1 crescent round into the waffle maker, using silicone tongs to stretch the round up the sides of the maker.
4. On top of the dough, layer 1/2 of the sliced steak, and 1/2 of the onions and peppers. Sprinkle with 2 tbsp grated cheese.
5. Add another crescent dough round to the top, stretching as needed to cover the edges. Close waffle maker and flip. Cook for 7 to 8 minutes.
6. Place the first stuffed waffle on a baking rack on a sheet pan and put in the oven to keep warm. Repeat with remaining ingredients spraying with cooking spray in between batches, if necessary.
7. Transfer the stuffed waffles to plates. Cut each in half and serve.

Chicken Pot Pie Waffle

Makes 2

1 tube	refrigerated crescent rolls
1 can	(18.8 oz) chicken pot pie

1. Preheat waffle maker. Preheat oven to 200°F.
2. Open the refrigerated crescent rolls and separate dough into 4 equal sections. Stretch each section into large circles to fit inside the waffle maker and up the sides.
3. Carefully add 1 crescent round into the waffle maker, using silicone tongs to stretch the round up the sides of the maker.
4. On top of the dough, ladle 1/2 cup chicken pot pie mixture.
5. Add another crescent round to the top, stretching as needed to cover the edges. Close waffle maker and flip. Cook for 7 to 8 minutes.
6. Place the first stuffed waffle on a baking rack on a sheet pan and put in the oven to keep warm. Repeat with remaining ingredients spraying with cooking spray in between batches, if necessary.
7. Transfer the stuffed waffles to plates. Ladle remaining chicken pot pie mixture over each. Serve warm.

Tuna Melt with Tomato Stuffed Waffle

Makes 1

2/3 cup	prepared waffle, pancake, or all-purpose baking mix 1/3 cup tuna salad (see recipe below)
1/4 cup	chopped Roma tomato
1	slice provolone cheese

1. Preheat waffle maker.
2. Spray waffle maker with cooking spray. Ladle about 1/3 cup batter into waffle maker, spreading batter so the bottom grids and waffle divider are thinly but completely covered.
3. Add tuna salad and chopped tomatoes to the top of the dough leaving a thin margin near the edge of the batter. Add provolone cheese on top.
4. Spread additional batter over filling until it reaches the top of the square projections on the waffle tongs. Close waffle maker and flip. Cook for 7 to 8 minutes.
5. Transfer stuffed waffle to a plate

Easy Tuna Salad

1	5 oz can albacore tuna in water, drained and flaked
1 tbsp	minced onion
2 tbsp	mayonnaise
1 tbsp	Dijon mustard
1 tsp	fresh lemon juice

Kosher salt and freshly ground black pepper

1. In a small bowl, mix tuna, onion, mayonnaise, mustard and lemon juice in a small bowl. Season to taste with salt and pepper.

International Flavors

Gyro Stuffed Waffle	68
Italian Melt Stuffed Waffle	69
Taco Waffles	71
Vegan Mediterranean Stuffed Waffle	72
Cubano-Style Stuffed Waffle	73
Bratwurst and Sauerkraut Stuffed Waffle	74

Gyro Stuffed Waffle

Makes 1

2/3 cup	Homestyle Belgian Waffle Batter
1 tsp	oregano
2 slices	gyro meat, preheated
2 tbsp	chopped tomato
1 thin slice	onion
	Tzatziki sauce, for serving

1. Preheat waffle maker.
2. Stir oregano into waffle batter.
3. Spray waffle maker with cooking spray. Ladle about 1/3 cup batter into waffle maker, spreading batter so the bottom grids and waffle divider are thinly but completely covered.
4. Arrange warm gyro slices and tomato in an even layer onto batter leaving a thin margin around edge. Separate onion slice into rings and arrange on top.
5. Spread additional batter over filling until it reaches the top of the square projections on the waffle tongs. Close waffle maker and flip. Cook for 7 to 8 minutes.
6. Transfer stuffed waffle to a plate. Serve with Tzatziki sauce.

Tips
* Tzatziki sauce can be found in the deli or produce department where dips and hummus are sold.

Taco Waffles

Makes 1

2/3 cup	Cornmeal Waffle Batter (recipe page xx)
2 tsp	minced jalapeño
1/4 cup	taco meat, cooked
3 tbsp	grated Mexican cheese blend
1 tbsp	salsa
	Sour cream (optional)

1. Preheat waffle maker.
2. Prepare Cornmeal Waffle Batter as directed in steps 1 to 4. Stir in the minced jalapeño.
3. Spray waffle maker with cooking spray. Ladle about 1/3 cup batter into waffle maker, spreading batter so the bottom grids and waffle divider are thinly but completely covered.
4. Spoon the taco meat, grated cheese and salsa evenly across the batter leaving about 1/4 inch space around the edge of the batter.
5. Pour the remaining batter on top of the filling and along the sides.
6. Close waffle maker and flip. Cook until golden brown and crisp, about 7 to 8 minutes.
7. Transfer the stuffed waffle to a plate. Serve with a dollop of sour cream, if using.

Tip

* If making more than one stuffed taco, preheat oven to 200°F. Place cooked waffles on a rack set on a baking sheet and put into the oven to keep warm until ready to serve.

Italian Melt Stuffed Waffle

Makes 1

2/3 cup	Classic Buttermilk Waffle Batter
1 tsp	Italian seasoning blend
1 slice	deli ham
3 slices	pepperoncini
1 slice	cotto salami
1 slice	Provolone cheese
	Pizza sauce for dipping (optional)

1. Preheat waffle maker.
2. Stir Italian seasoning blend into waffle batter.
3. Spray waffle maker with cooking spray. Ladle about 1/3 cup batter into waffle maker, spreading batter so the bottom grids and waffle divider are thinly but completely covered.
4. Arrange deli ham, pepperoncini, cotto salami and Provolone cheese in an even layer onto batter leaving a thin margin around edge.
5. Spread additional batter over filling until it reaches the top of the square projections on the waffle tongs. Close waffle maker and flip. Cook for 7 to 8 minutes.
6. Transfer stuffed waffle to a plate. Cut waffles into wedges and serve with Pizza sauce, if using.

Vegan Mediterranean Stuffed Waffle

Makes 1

2/3 cup	Vegan Chickpea Waffles
	Spinach leaves
2	roasted red pepper strips
3 slices	cucumber
2 tbsp	sliced black olives
2 tbsp	crumbled feta cheese

1. Preheat waffle maker.
2. Spray waffle maker with cooking spray. Ladle about 1/3 cup batter into waffle maker, spreading batter so the bottom grids and waffle divider are thinly but completely covered.
3. Arrange spinach leaves, roasted red peppers, cucumber and black olives in an even layer onto batter leaving a thin margin around edge. Sprinkle with the feta cheese.
4. Spread additional batter over filling until it reaches the top of the square projections on the waffle tongs. Close waffle maker and flip. Cook for 7 to 8 minutes.
5. Transfer stuffed waffle to a plate. Cut waffles into wedges and serve.

Cubano-Style Stuffed Waffle

Makes 4

1 tube	refrigerated crescent dough
4 slices	roasted pork
4 tsp	yellow mustard
4 sliced	deli ham
4	dill pickle planks
8 slices	Swiss cheese

1. Preheat waffle maker. Preheat oven to 200°F.
2. Open the refrigerated biscuit tube and separate biscuits into 8 pieces. Stretch biscuits into large circles to fit inside the waffle maker and up the sides.
3. Carefully add 1 biscuit round into the waffle maker, using silicone tongs to stretch the round up the sides of the maker. Spread 1 tsp on each of the roasted pork slices. Place 1 pork slice on top of the biscuit dough leaving a thin margin around edge. Add 1 slice deli ham, 1 dill pickle plank, and 2 slices of Swiss cheese.
4. Add 1 biscuit round to the top, stretching as needed to cover the edges. Close waffle maker and flip. Cook for 7 to 8 minutes.
5. Place the first stuffed waffle on a baking rack on a sheet pan and put in the oven to keep warm. Repeat with remaining ingredients spraying with cooking spray in between batches, if necessary.
6. Transfer the stuffed waffles to plates. Cut into halves or quarters as desired.

Tips
* All-purpose baking mixes can be substituted for refrigerated dough. Prepare as directed on package. The yield may vary depending on the mix used
* This recipe makes 4 stuffed waffles as leftover refrigerator biscuit dough does not store well.
* You can refrigerate cooked stuffed waffles in a tightly sealed container in the refrigerator up to 3 days.

Bratwurst and Sauerkraut Stuffed Waffle

Makes 1

2/3 cup	Homestyle Belgian Waffle Batter
1	cooked bratwurst, thinly sliced
2 tbsp	sauerkraut
	Spicy brown mustard, for serving

1. Preheat waffle maker.
2. Spray waffle maker with cooking spray. Ladle about 1/3 cup batter into waffle maker, spreading batter so the bottom grids and waffle divider are thinly but completely covered.
3. Place bratwurst slices onto batter leaving a thin margin around edge. Add sauerkraut over bratwurst.
4. Spread additional batter over filling until it reaches the top of the square projections on the waffle tongs. Close waffle maker and flip. Cook for 7 to 8 minutes.
5. Transfer stuffed waffle to a plate. Serve with spicy brown mustard.

Desserts

Banana Split Stuffed Chocolate Waffle	77
Cherry Pie Stuffed Waffle	78
Pear and Lemon Curd Stuffed Waffles	79
Peach Pie Stuffed Waffle	81
Pineapple Upside Down Stuffed Waffle	82
Pumpkin Cheesecake Stuffed Waffle	83
Turtle Cheesecake Stuffed Waffle	84

Banana Split Stuffed Chocolate Waffle

Makes 1

2/3 cup	prepared Homestyle Buttermilk Waffles
1 tbsp	cocoa powder
1 tsp	granulated sugar
1/2 tsp	vanilla extract
1/4 cup	sliced banana
1/4 cup	sliced maraschino cherries
1 tbsp	chocolate chips
	Whipped cream (optional)

1. Preheat waffle maker.
2. Stir cocoa powder, granulated sugar and vanilla extract into waffle batter.
3. Spray waffle maker with cooking spray. Ladle about 1/3 cup batter into waffle maker, spreading batter so the bottom grids and waffle divider are thinly but completely covered.
4. Arrange sliced bananas and maraschino cherries in an even layer onto batter leaving a thin margin around edge. Sprinkle with chocolate chips.
5. Spread additional batter over filling until it reaches the top of the square projections on the waffle tongs. Close waffle maker and flip. Cook for 7 to 8 minutes.
6. Transfer stuffed waffle to a plate. Cut waffles into wedges and serve with a dollop of whipped cream, if using.

Cherry Pie Stuffed Waffle

Makes 1

2/3 cup	prepared Homestyle Buttermilk Waffles
1/2 cup	cherry pie filling
	Whipped cream topping (optional)

1. Preheat waffle maker.
2. Spray waffle maker with cooking spray. Ladle about 1/3 cup batter into waffle maker, spreading batter so the bottom grids and waffle divider are thinly but completely covered.
3. Spoon cherry pie filling onto batter leaving a thin margin around edge.
4. Spread additional batter over filling until it reaches the top of the square projections on the waffle tongs. Close waffle maker and flip. Cook for 7 to 8 minutes.
5. Transfer stuffed waffle to a plate. Serve with a dollop of whipped cream, if using.

Tip
* A can of cherry pie filling is typically 21 oz. You will get about 4 servings from one can of filling.
* You can store leftover pie filling in a tightly sealed container in the refrigerator for 1 to 2 days. Do not store it in its original can.

Pear and Lemon Curd Stuffed Waffles

Makes 1 serving

2/3 cup	prepared box (15-ounce) of Gingerbread Cake and Cookie Mix
1/2 cup	sliced pear
	Lemon curd, for serving

1. Preheat waffle maker.
2. Prepare Gingerbread Cake according to the package directions.
3. Spray waffle maker with cooking spray. Ladle about 1/3 cup batter into waffle maker, spreading batter so the bottom grids and waffle divider are thinly but completely covered.
4. Arrange sliced pears in an even layer onto batter leaving a thin margin around edge. Sprinkle with chocolate chips.
5. Spread additional batter over filling until it reaches the top of the square projections on the waffle tongs. Close waffle maker and flip. Cook for 7 to 8 minutes.
6. Transfer stuffed waffle to a plate. Cut waffles into wedges and serve a spoonful of lemon curd on top.

Tips
* 1 small pear will yield about the 1/2 cup needed for this recipe. A medium pear yields about 3/4 cup and a large pear yields about 1-1/4 cups. Do not overstuff the waffle if you have more pears. You can serve them on the side or top.
* The leftover cake batter can be refrigerated in an airtight container for 1 to 2 days.
* You can also use the cake batter to make more stuffed waffles or plain, unstuffed waffles.

Peach Pie Stuffed Waffle

Makes 1

2/3 cup	prepared Homestyle Buttermilk Waffles
1/2 tsp	ground cinnamon
1/2 cup	peach pie filling
1 tbsp	chopped pecans
	Whipped cream topping (optional)

1. Preheat waffle maker.
2. Stir ground cinnamon into waffle batter.
3. Spray waffle maker with cooking spray. Ladle about 1/3 cup batter into waffle maker, spreading batter so the bottom grids and waffle divider are thinly but completely covered.
4. Spoon peach pie filling onto batter leaving a thin margin around edge. Sprinkle with chopped pecans.
5. Spread additional batter over filling until it reaches the top of the square projections on the waffle tongs. Close waffle maker and flip. Cook for 7 to 8 minutes.
6. Transfer stuffed waffle to a plate. Cut waffles into wedges and serve with a dollop of whipped cream, if using.

Tip
* A can of peach pie filling is typically 21 oz. You will get about 4 servings from one can of filling.
* You can store leftover pie filling in a tightly sealed container in the refrigerator for 1 to 2 days. Do not store it in its original can.

Pineapple Upside Down Stuffed Waffle

Makes 1

2/3 cup	prepared Pancake and Waffle mix
1/2 cup	canned pineapple chunks in water, drained
2	maraschino cherries, halved
1 tbsp	brown sugar

1. Preheat waffle maker.
2. Spray waffle maker with cooking spray. Ladle about 1/3 cup batter into waffle maker, spreading batter so the bottom grids and waffle divider are thinly but completely covered.
3. Arrange pineapple chunks and maraschino cherries onto batter leaving a thin margin around edge. Sprinkle with brown sugar.
4. Spread additional batter over filling until it reaches the top of the square projections on the waffle tongs. Close waffle maker and flip. Cook for 7 to 8 minutes.
5. Transfer stuffed waffle to a plate. Cut into wedges and serve.

Tip
* Serve leftover pineapple chunks on the side.

Pumpkin Cheesecake Stuffed Waffle

Makes 1

2/3 cup	prepared box (15-ounce) of Pumpkin Cake Mix
1/4 cup	refrigerated no-bake cheesecake filling, softened
3 tbsp	chopped pecans
	Cream cheese frosting (optional)

1. Preheat waffle maker.
2. Prepare Pumpkin Cake Mix according to the package directions.
3. Spray waffle maker with cooking spray. Ladle about 1/3 cup batter into waffle maker, spreading batter so the bottom grids and waffle divider are thinly but completely covered.
4. Spoon cheesecake filling onto batter leaving a thin margin around edge. Sprinkle with chopped pecans.
5. Spread additional batter over filling until it reaches the top of the square projections on the waffle tongs. Close waffle maker and flip. Cook for 7 to 8 minutes.
6. Transfer stuffed waffle to a plate. Spread waffle with cream cheese frosting. Cut waffles into wedges and serve.

Tips
* The leftover cake batter can be refrigerated in an airtight container for 1 to 2 days.
* You can also use the cake batter to make more stuffed waffles or plain, unstuffed waffles.
* Cream cheese frosting can be found in a can near the cake mix in grocery stores.

Turtle Cheesecake Stuffed Waffle

Makes 1

1	prepared package (15-ounce) Chocolate Cake Mix
1/4 cup	refrigerated no-bake cheesecake filling
2 tbsp	chopped pecans
2 tbsp	chocolate chips Caramel sauce

1. Preheat waffle maker.
2. Prepare Chocolate Cake Mix according to the package directions.
3. Spray waffle maker with cooking spray. Ladle about 1/3 cup batter into waffle maker, spreading batter so the bottom grids and waffle divider are thinly but completely covered.
4. Spoon cheesecake filling onto batter leaving a thin margin around edge. Sprinkle with chopped pecans and chocolate chips.
5. Spread additional batter over filling until it reaches the top of the square projections on the waffle tongs. Close waffle maker and flip. Cook for 7 to 8 minutes.
6. Transfer stuffed waffle to a plate. Drizzle waffle with caramel sauce.

Tips
* The leftover cake batter can be refrigerated in an airtight container for 1 to 2 days.
* You can also use the cake batter to make more stuffed waffles or plain, unstuffed waffles.
* You can find caramel sauce either in the cake mix section or near the ice cream freezer section in your grocery store. Often, the sauce near the ice cream is a squirt bottle making it easy to drizzle.

Kid-Friendly

Ballpark Corn Dog Stuffed Waffle	**86**
Favorite Mac 'n Cheese Stuffed Waffle	**87**
Crunchy Apple Peanut Butter Stuffed Waffle	**89**
S'mores Stuffed Waffle	**91**
Oreo Stuffed Waffles	**92**

Ballpark Corn Dog Stuffed Waffle

Makes 1

2/3 cup	Cornmeal Waffle Batter
1	hot dog, sliced lengthwise and then in 1-1/2 inch pieces.
	Ketchup and mustard for serving

1. Preheat waffle maker.
2. Spray waffle maker with cooking spray. Ladle about 1/3 cup batter into waffle maker, spreading batter so the bottom grids and waffle divider are thinly but completely covered.
3. Arrange hot dog pieces on top of the batter leaving a thin margin around edge.
4. Spread additional batter over filling until it reaches the top of the square projections on the waffle tongs. Close waffle maker and flip. Cook for 7 to 8 minutes.
5. Transfer stuffed waffle to a plate. Serve with ketchup and mustard.

Tip
* Use quality hot dogs/weiners for the best result.

Variations
* Use any flavored hot dog you prefer. Options such as beef, turkey, pork, chicken, cheese stuffed and more all work great in this recipe.
* For a vegetarian option, use plant-based hot dogs.
* Use boxed cornbread mix and prepare according to the package directions.

Favorite Mac 'n Cheese Stuffed Waffle

Makes 1

2/3 cup	Classic Buttermilk Waffle Batter
1/2 cup	leftover macaroni and cheese

1. Preheat waffle maker.
2. Spray waffle maker with cooking spray. Ladle about 1/3 cup batter into waffle maker, spreading batter so the bottom grids and waffle divider are thinly but completely covered.
3. Spoon macaroni and cheese on to the batter leaving a thin margin around the edge.
4. Spread additional batter over filling until it reaches the top of the square projections on the waffle tongs. Close waffle maker and flip. Cook for 7 to 8 minutes.
5. Transfer stuffed waffle to a plate.

Tip

* If you are making macaroni and cheese instead of using leftovers, refrigerate the macaroni and cheese before using. This will help the macaroni firm up before waffling.

Crunchy Apple Peanut Butter Stuffed Waffle

Makes 1

2/3 cup	prepared Pancake and Waffle mix
1/2 cup	medium-diced apple (about 1 medium apple)
1/2 tsp	granulated sugar
1/8 tsp	ground cinnamon
2 tbsp	extra crunchy peanut butter
2 tbsp	cream cheese, softened

1. Preheat waffle maker.
2. In a small bowl, add the diced apples and sprinkle with sugar and cinnamon. Toss to coat. Set aside.
3. Prepare waffle batter as directed on package.
4. In another small bowl, combine the peanut butter and the cream cheese.
5. Spray waffle maker with cooking spray. Ladle about 1/3 cup batter into waffle maker, spreading batter so the bottom grids and waffle divider are thinly but completely covered.
6. Scatter apples top of the batter leaving a thin margin around edge. Top with dollops of the peanut butter and cream cheese mixture.
7. Spread additional batter over filling until it reaches the top of the square projections on the waffle tongs. Close waffle maker and flip. Cook for 7 to 8 minutes.
8. Transfer stuffed waffle to a plate. Serve cut into quarters.

Tips
* Choose apples such as Honeycrisp, Granny Smith, Braeburn or Golden Delicious for the best results.
* Feel free to use other varieties of peanut butter instead of the extra- crunchy. Do not use an all-natural peanut butter as they can contain more liquids.

S'mores Stuffed Waffle

Makes 1

2/3 cup	Classic Buttermilk Waffle Batter
1/4 cup	chocolate chips
2 tbsp	crushed graham crackers
2 tbsp	marshmallow cream

1. Preheat waffle maker.
2. Spray waffle maker with cooking spray. Ladle about 1/3 cup batter into waffle maker, spreading batter so the bottom grids and waffle divider are thinly but completely covered.
3. Scatter chocolate chips and crushed graham crackers on top of the batter leaving a thin margin around edge. Drop small spoons of marshmallow cream all over the top.
4. Spread additional batter over filling until it reaches the top of the square projections on the waffle tongs. Close waffle maker and flip. Cook for 7 to 8 minutes.
5. Transfer stuffed waffle to a plate. Serve cut into quarters.

Variations
* Mallow Cups can be used in place of chocolate chips and marshmallow cream.
* *Peanut Butter Cup Waffles:* Use peanut butter cups in place of the chocolate chips and marshmallow cream.

Tip
* Waffle, pancake, or all-purpose baking mixes can be substituted for Classic Waffle Batter recipe. Prepare as directed on package. Yield may vary depending on the mix used.

Oreo Stuffed Waffles

Makes 2

1 tube	(8 count) refrigerated Crescent Rolls
1	Oreo cookies, crumbled
	Cold milk (because of course you need cold milk with Oreo Cookies!)

1. Preheat waffle maker. Preheat oven to 200°F.
2. Open the refrigerated crescent roll tube and separate dough into 4 pieces. Stretch crescent dough into large circles to fit inside the waffle maker and up the sides.
3. Carefully add 1 crescent round into the waffle maker, using silicone tongs to stretch the round up the sides of the maker. Add one Oreo cookie on top of the dough.
4. Add 1 crescent dough round to the top, stretching as needed to cover the edges. Close waffle maker and flip. Cook for 7 to 8 minutes.
5. Place the first stuffed waffle on a baking rack on a sheet pan and put in the oven to keep warm. Repeat with remaining ingredients spraying with cooking spray in between batches, if necessary.
6. Transfer the stuffed waffles to plates. Serve with a glass of cold milk for dipping.

Tip
* To crumble Oreos, place them in a plastic bag and gently pound them with the bottom of a glass or other firm object.
* Unlike many of the other recipes in this book, this one makes 4 stuffed waffles as leftover refrigerator biscuit dough does not store well.
* You can refrigerate cooked stuffed waffles in a tightly sealed container in the refrigerator up to 3 days.

Seasonal

Christmas Candy Stuffed Waffle	95
Valentine Cherry Chocolate Stuffed Waffle	97
St. Paddy's Day Corned Beef Stuffed Waffle	98
Easter Carrot Cake Stuffed Waffle	99
Independence Day Confetti Cake Waffle	101
Thanksgiving Leftovers Stuffed Waffle	102
New Year's Good Luck Stuffed Waffle	103

Christmas Candy Stuffed Waffle

Makes 1

2/3 cup	Classic Waffle Batter
2 tsp	green and red sprinkles
1 oz	chocolate bar (about 1/4 cup), broken into pieces
1 tbsp	crushed candy cane (about one 5-inch candy cane)
1 tbsp	chopped pecans

1. Preheat waffle maker.
2. Spray waffle maker with cooking spray. Ladle about 1/3 cup batter into waffle maker, spreading batter so the bottom grids and waffle divider are thinly but completely covered.
3. Scatter chocolate pieces, crushed candy cane and chopped on top of the batter leaving a thin margin around edge. Drop small spoons of marshmallow cream all over the top.
4. Spread additional batter over filling until it reaches the top of the square projections on the waffle tongs. Close waffle maker and flip. Cook for 7 to 8 minutes.
5. Transfer stuffed waffle to a plate. Serve cut into quarters.

Valentine Cherry Chocolate Stuffed Waffle

Makes 2

1	prepared package (15-ounce) Chocolate Cake Mix
1/2 cup	ricotta cheese
1/4 cup	chocolate chips
2 tbsp	chopped maraschino cherries
2 tsp	maraschino cherry juice
	Whipped cream topping (optional)

1. Preheat waffle maker. Preheat oven to 200°F.
2. Prepare Chocolate Cake Mix according to the package directions.
3. Spray waffle maker with cooking spray. Ladle about 1/3 cup batter into waffle maker, spreading batter so the bottom grids and waffle divider are thinly but completely covered.
4. In a small bowl, combine ricotta cheese, chocolate chips, the chopped maraschino cherries and juice. Spoon one half the mixture onto batter leaving a thin margin around edge.
5. Spread additional batter over filling until it reaches the top of the square projections on the waffle tongs. Close waffle maker and flip. Cook for 7 to 8 minutes.
6. Place the first stuffed waffle on a baking rack on a sheet pan and put in the oven to keep warm. Repeat with remaining ingredients spraying with cooking spray in between batches, if necessary.
7. Transfer stuffed waffles to plates. Top with a dollop of sour cream, if using.

Tips
* The leftover cake batter can be refrigerated in an airtight container for 1 to 2 days.
* You can also use the cake batter to make more stuffed waffles or plain, unstuffed waffles.

St. Paddy's Day Corned Beef Stuffed Waffle

Makes 1

2/3 cup	prepared pancake and waffle
2	thin slices cooked corned beef
1 tsp	whole grain mustard
	Additional mustard for dipping

1. Preheat waffle maker.
2. Spray waffle maker with cooking spray. Ladle about 1/3 cup batter into waffle maker, spreading batter so the bottom grids and waffle divider are thinly but completely covered.
3. Arrange corned beef slices on top of batter leaving a thin margin around the edges. Add mustard and using the back of a spoon, spread the mustard over the top of the corned beef.
4. Spread additional batter over filling until it reaches the top of the square projections on the waffle tongs. Close waffle maker and flip. Cook for 7 to 8 minutes.
5. Transfer stuffed waffles to plates.

Tip
* Corned beef can be found in the deli section of your supermarket.

Variations
* Substitute pastrami for the corned beef if desired.
* Substitute your favorite mustard for the whole grain mustard.

Easter Carrot Cake Stuffed Waffle

Makes 1

1	prepared package (15-ounce) Carrot Cake Mix
2 oz	cream cheese, softened
1 tsp	honey
2 tbsp	raisins, divided
	Cream cheese frosting (optional)

1. Preheat waffle maker.
2. Prepare Carrot Cake Mix according to the package directions.
3. Spray waffle maker with cooking spray. Ladle about 1/3 cup batter into waffle maker, spreading batter so the bottom grids and waffle divider are thinly but completely covered.
4. In a small bowl, combine cream cheese, honey and 1/2 the raisins. Spoon the mixture onto batter leaving a thin margin around edge. Top with the remaining raisins.
5. Spread additional batter over filling until it reaches the top of the square projections on the waffle tongs. Close waffle maker and flip. Cook for 7 to 8 minutes.
6. Transfer stuffed waffle to a plate. Spread the top with cream cheese frosting, if using.

Tips
* The leftover cake batter can be refrigerated in an airtight container for 1 to 2 days.
* You can also use the cake batter to make more stuffed waffles or plain, unstuffed waffles.

Independence Day Confetti Cake Waffle

Makes 4

1 box	white confetti cake batter, prepared according to the instructions on the package
1 cup	candy sprinkles
1 can	(16 oz) vanilla frosting

1. Preheat waffle maker. Preheat oven to 200°F.
2. Spray waffle maker with cooking spray.
3. Add 1/3 cup cake batter to the stuffed waffle maker. Spoon 2 tbsp vanilla frosting on top of the batter. Sprinkle with 1 tbsp sprinkles
4. Add 1/3 cup cake batter to the top of the filling. Close waffle maker and flip. Cook until golden brown and crisp, about 8 to 10 minutes.
5. Place waffle on a baking rack on a sheet pan and put in the oven to keep warm. Repeat with remaining ingredients, spraying with cooking spray in between.
6. Transfer the stuffed waffles to a plate.
7. Let the waffles cool before adding the frosting. Spread remaining frosting, equally divided over the top of the waffles. Sprinkle each with remaining candy sprinkles.
8. Cut into quarters and serve.

Variation
* Instead of the confetti cake, use the Classic Waffle Batter add 1/2 cup candy sprinkles to the batter.

Thanksgiving Leftovers Stuffed Waffle
Makes 2

3 cups	prepared stuffing, homemade or prepackaged mix (see Tip)
2	large eggs, beaten
	Chicken broth or turkey stock, if necessary
1 cup	sliced leftover turkey
1/2 cup	leftover cranberry sauce Gravy

1. Preheat waffle maker. Preheat oven to 200°F.
2. In a large bowl, mix together stuffing and eggs. If stuffing is dry, add chicken broth 1 tbsp at a time until stuffing is moist, but only up to 8 tbsp broth.
3. Scoop 1 cup of the waffle mixture into waffle maker. With rubber spatula, spread evenly on the bottom and up along the sides
4. Fill with 1/2 cup turkey leaving a thin margin around edge. Layer in 1/4 cup cranberry sauce.
5. Top with about 1/3 cup of additional waffle mixture. Using a spatula to move mixture to side to completely cover the turkey and cranberries. Close waffle maker and flip. Cook for 8 to 9 minutes.
6. Place the first stuffed waffle on a baking rack on a sheet pan and put in the oven to keep warm. Repeat with remaining ingredients spraying with cooking spray in between batches, if necessary.
7. Remove stuffed waffled to plated. Let waffle stand for 3 minutes before cutting. Serve with gravy on the side.

Tips
* Do not use stuffing with chunks of vegetables, sausage, oysters or dried fruit.

New Year's Good Luck Stuffed Waffle

There's an old southern saying that eating black eyed peas on New Years bring good luck. Stuffed waffles are a great place to start the new year.
Year.

Makes 3

1	prepared Cornbread Waffle Batter (page 16)
1 can	(14.5 oz) Southern-style black eyed peas

1. Preheat waffle maker. Preheat oven to 200°F.
2. Spray waffle maker with cooking spray. Ladle about 1/3 cup batter into waffle maker, spreading batter so the bottom grids and waffle divider are thinly but completely covered.
3. Ladle 1/2 cup black eyed peas on top of the batter.
4. Spread additional batter over filling until it reaches the top of the square projections on the waffle tongs. Close waffle maker and flip. Cook for 7 to 8 minutes.
5. Place the first stuffed waffle on a baking rack on a sheet pan and put in the oven to keep warm. Repeat with remaining ingredients spraying with cooking spray in between batches, if necessary.
6. Transfer stuffed waffles to plates.

From the Author

I cannot thank you enough for your interest in my Egg Bites Cookbook. I sincerely hope you have found recipes that you love and will keep as your favorites. Even more, I hope I have made making a quick and delicious breakfast much easier for you.
If you would like to get more recipes and easy, delicious recipes, join me at SmashingEats.com

Check out more of my #1 Best Selling Cookbooks on Amazon.
I would love to hear from you. If you like the recipes you've tried and would recommend these to others, please write a review on Amazon.com

I appreciate you being my customer!

Thank you, Marilyn

Made in United States
Troutdale, OR
05/21/2025

31586707R00062